GW00359550

When

Spiritual reflections from the second year of
the Pontificate of Benedict XVI

Edited by
Lucio Coco

*All booklets are published thanks to the
generous support of the members of the
Catholic Truth Society*

CATHOLIC TRUTH SOCIETY
PUBLISHERS TO THE HOLY SEE

Foreword

This anthology is composed of reflections drawn from the addresses and writings of the Holy Father, Benedict XVI. The editor offers us a short thesaurus; as a precious spring where we may take light and strength for the daily journey.

Each thought of the collection is like the nectar collected from a flower garden in full bloom; it impregnates the heart with a sweet scent. It is the scent of Christ, and it offers us a path to follow him on the way of truth and love.

Men and women in our times are surrounded by too many superfluous things that are unable to produce happiness. Jesus is the only necessary One they are missing. The words of Pope Benedict XVI continually guide our gaze towards Him. The Holy Father has passionately sought Him out throughout his life and he can rightly say with St Paul that for him life is Christ. He is able to communicate to us his real life and deep experience of Jesus Christ: "To the extent that we nourish ourselves on Christ and are in love with him, we feel within us the incentive to bring others to him: indeed, we cannot keep the joy of the faith to ourselves; we must pass it on. This need becomes even stronger and more pressing in the context of that strange forgetfulness of God which has spread in vast areas of the world today" (n. 68).

These vast areas of the world are arid and desolate, they are deprived of life and hope. It is urgent that they be revived. To do so is the task of those who have the grace and joy of believing.

These reflections are like drops of heavenly dew flowing from the heart of Pope Benedict XVI; a heart in love with Jesus Christ. May they awaken in numerous other hearts the desire to know Him who is our Life and who continuously communicates to us through his Word, the sacrifice of the Cross and the Eucharist. This last, what the Holy Father calls "the sacrament of love", is the Bread which sustains us on the earthly journey towards the heavenly Jerusalem. It is the city of eternal peace that every human heart, knowingly or not, desires to reach.

Mother Anna Cànopi OSB

April 2006

1. The eyes of love

There is a profound unity between truth and good, between the eyes of the mind and those of the heart: *"Ubi amor, ibi oculos"*, Riccardo di San Vittore said, ...love makes one see.

Address to Congregation for Catholic Education

(April 1, 2006)

2. Building Europe

Man cannot understand himself fully if he ignores God. This is the reason why, at the time when the Europe of the third millennium is being built, the religious dimension of human existence cannot be neglected.

Address to Congregation for Catholic Education

(April 1, 2006)

3. Creature

A human being's value does not depend on his efficiency or appearance but on himself, because he was created and loved by God.

Address on the first anniversary of the death of John Paul II (April 2, 2006)

4. Encounter

If a person allows himself to be embraced by Christ, he does not repress the riches of his humanity; if he adheres to Christ with all his heart, he will never lack anything.

Address on the first anniversary of the death of John Paul II (April 2, 2006)

5. Trial

In life's difficulties it is especially the quality of the faith of each one of us that is tried and tested: its firmness, its purity, its consistency with life.

Homily on the first anniversary of the death of John Paul II (April 3, 2006)

6. Lectio divina

One must not read Sacred Scripture as one reads any kind of historical book, such as, for example, Homer, Ovid or Horace; it is necessary truly to read it as the Word of God, that is, entering into a conversation with God. One must start by praying and talking to the Lord: "Open the door to me".

Answering young people preparing for WYD

(April 6, 2006)

7. Sacrifice

We all know that to reach a goal in a sport or in one's profession, discipline and sacrifices are required; but then, by reaching a desired goal, it is all crowned with success. Life itself is like this. In other words, becoming men and women according to Jesus' plan demands sacrifices, but these are by no means negative; on the contrary, they are a help in living as people with new hearts, in living a truly human and happy life.

Answering young people preparing for WYD

(April 6, 2006)

8. Gift of love

We must make God present again in our society. This seems to me to be the first essential element: that God be once again present in our lives, that we do not live as though we were autonomous, authorised to invent what freedom and life are. We must realise that we are creatures, aware that there is a God who has created us and that living in accordance with his will is not dependence but a gift of love that makes us alive.

Answering young people preparing for WYD

(April 6, 2006)

9. "What God?"

There are so many false images of God, a violent God... The point, therefore, is recognising God who has shown us his face in Jesus, who suffered for us, who loved us to the point of dying, and thus overcame violence. It is necessary to make the living God present in our "own" lives first of all, the God who is not a stranger, a fictitious God, a God only thought of, but a God who has shown himself, who has shown his being and his face. Only in this way do our lives become true, authentically human.

Answering young people preparing for WYD

(April 6, 2006)

10. Friendship with Jesus

It is necessary to enter into real friendship with Jesus in a personal relationship with him and not to know who Jesus is only from others or from books, but to live an ever deeper personal relationship with Jesus, where we can begin to understand what he is asking of us. The awareness of what I am, of my possibilities: on the one hand, courage, and on the other, humility, trust and openness.

Answering young people preparing for WYD

(April 6, 2006)

11. A great adventure

What does the Lord want of me? Of course, this is always a great adventure, but life can be successful only if we have the courage to be adventurous, trusting that the Lord will never leave me alone, that the Lord will go with me and help me.

Answering young people preparing for WYD

(April 6, 2006)

12. Evil

The true problem challenging faith today seems to me to be the evil in the world: we ask ourselves how it can be compatible with the Creator's rationality. And here we truly need God, who was made flesh and shows us that he is not only a mathematical reason but that this original Reason is also Love.

Answering young people preparing for WYD

(April 6, 2006)

13. Interior freedom

The poverty that Jesus means - that the prophets mean - presupposes above all inner freedom from greed for possession and the mania for power ... Inner freedom is the prerequisite for overcoming the corruption and greed that devastate the world today. This freedom can only be found if God becomes our richness; it can only be found in the patience of daily sacrifices, in which, as it were, true freedom develops.

Homily for the Mass of Palm Sunday (April 9, 2006)

14. The sign of the cross

Every time we make the Sign of the Cross we should remember not to confront injustice with other injustice or violence with other violence: let us remember that we can only overcome evil with good and never by paying evil back with evil.

Homily for the Mass of Palm Sunday (April 9, 2006)

15. Giving oneself

We do not find life by possessing it, but by giving it.

Homily for the Mass of Palm Sunday (April 9, 2006)

16. To young people

Never forget, dear young people, that in the end your happiness, our happiness, depends on the encounter with Jesus and on friendship with him.

Address to Meeting of "UNIV 2006" (April 10, 2006)

17. Understanding

It is great to feel oneself understood by another and to begin to understand the other person.
Address to Meeting of "UNIV 2006" (April 10, 2006)

18. Overcoming

It is true: the Cross shows "the breadth and length and height and depth" - the cosmic dimensions is the meaning - of a love that surpasses all knowledge, a love that goes beyond what is known and fills us "with all the fullness of God" (*Ep* 3:18-19).
General audience (April 12, 2006)

19. Reconciliation

The forgiveness which Christ gives to us in the Sacrament of Penance is a source of interior and exterior peace and makes us apostles of peace in a world where divisions, suffering and the tragedies of injustice, hatred and violence and the inability to be reconciled to one another in order to start again with a sincere pardon, unfortunately continue.
General audience (April 12, 2006)

20. Lectio et oratio

The reading of Sacred Scripture is prayer, it must be prayer - it must emerge from prayer and lead to prayer.
Homily for the Chrism Mass (April 13, 2006)

21. Friend of Jesus

This is the profound meaning of being a priest: becoming the friend of Jesus Christ. For this friendship we must daily recommit ourselves.
Homily for the Chrism Mass (April 13, 2006)

22. The fall

God loves his creature, man; he even loves him in his fall and does not leave him to himself. He loves him to the end. He is impelled with his love to the very end, to the extreme: he came down from his divine glory. He cast aside the raiment of his divine glory and put on the garb of a slave. He came down to the extreme lowliness of our fall.
Homily for the Mass "In Coena Domini" (April 13, 2006)

23. The holiness of God

God is not a remote God, too distant or too great to be bothered with our trifles. Since God is great, he can also be concerned with small things. Since he is great, the soul of man, the same man, created through eternal love, is not a small thing but great, and worthy of God's love. God's holiness is not merely an incandescent power before which we are obliged to withdraw, terrified. It is a power of love and therefore a purifying and healing power.
Homily for the Mass "In Coena Domini" (April 13, 2006)

24. The sin of pride

What is it that makes man unclean? It is the rejection of love, not wanting to be loved, not loving. It is pride that believes it has no need of any purification, that is closed to God's saving goodness. It is pride that does not want to admit or recognise that we are in need of purification.
Homily for the Mass "In Coena Domini" (April 13, 2006)

25. The way of the cross

Life comes to us from being loved by him who is Life; it comes to us from living-with and loving-with him. I, but no longer I: this is the way of the Cross, the way that "crosses over" a life simply closed in on the I, thereby opening up the road towards true and lasting joy.
Homily for the Paschal Vigil (April 15, 2006)

26. Believing in order to see

Those who meet the Risen Jesus are inwardly transformed; it is impossible "to see" the Risen One without "believing" in him. Let us pray that he will call each one of us by name and thus convert us, opening us to the "vision" of faith.
General audience (April 19, 2006)

27. Spiritual music

By raising the soul to contemplation, music also helps us grasp the most intimate nuances of human genius, in which is reflected something of the

incomparable beauty of the Creator of the universe.
Address at first anniversary concert (April 21, 2006)

28. Tradition

Tradition is not merely the material transmission of what was given at the beginning to the Apostles, but the effective presence of the Crucified and Risen Lord Jesus who accompanies and guides in the Spirit the community he has gathered together… Tradition is the living river that links us to the origins, the living river in which the origins are ever present; the great river that leads us to the gates of eternity.
General audience (April 26, 2006)

29. Secular morals and Christian morals

Some have reached the point of theorising on the absolute sovereignty of reason and freedom in the context of moral norms: they presume that these norms constitute the context of a purely "human" ethic, in other words, the expression of a law that man makes for himself by himself. The advocates of this "secular morality" say that man as a rational being not only can but must decide freely on the value of his behavior … God's law correctly interpreted neither attenuates nor, even less, eliminates man's freedom. On the contrary, it guarantees and fosters this freedom because, as the Catechism of the Catholic Church reminds us, "freedom ... attains its perfection when directed toward God, our beatitude" (n. 1731). The moral law established by God in creation and confirmed in the Old Testament revelation reaches fulfilment and greatness in Christ. Jesus Christ is the way of perfection, the living and personal synthesis of perfect freedom in total obedience to God's will.

Address Pontifical Biblical Commission (April 27, 2006)

30. Eclipse of transcendence

Many children now grow up in a society which is forgetful of God and of the innate dignity of the human person made in God's image. In a world shaped by the accelerating processes of globalisation, they are often exposed solely to materialistic visions of the universe, of life and human fulfillment. Yet children and young people are by nature receptive, generous, idealistic and open to transcendence. They need above all else to be exposed to love and to develop in a healthy human ecology, where they can come to realise that they have not been cast into the world by chance, but through a gift that is part of God's loving plan.

Letter to Pontifical Academy of Social Sciences
(April 27, 2006)

May 2006

31. Our mother

Here, together with salvation, we felt ourselves anticipating, in the words of the elderly Simeon, the contradictory sign of the Cross, and of the sword that beneath the Cross of the Son was to pierce the Mother's soul, thereby making her not only the Mother of God but also Mother of us all.

Visit to the Roman Shrine of Divine Love (May 1, 2006)

32. Friends of God

Wisdom forms people, making them grow from within towards the full stature of their maturity; and it contextually affirms that this fullness of life consists in friendship with God, in an intimate harmony with his being and his will. The interior place in which Divine Wisdom operates is what the Bible calls "the heart", the person's spiritual centre.

Homily, Fifth Centenary of the Swiss Guard (May 6, 2006)

33. The priest and the cross

The only legitimate ascent towards the shepherd's ministry is the Cross. This is the true way to rise; this is the true door. It is not the desire to become "someone" for oneself, but rather to exist for others, for Christ, and thus through him and with him to be there for the people he seeks, whom he wants to lead on the path of life. One enters the priesthood through the Sacrament, and this means precisely: through the gift of oneself to Christ, so that he can make use of me; so that I may serve him and follow his call, even if it proves contrary to my desire for self-fulfillment and esteem.

Homily at the ordination of 15 priests (May 7, 2006)

34. Day by day

Life is not only given at the moment of death and not only in the manner of martyrdom. We must give it day by day. Day after day it is necessary to learn that I do not possess my life for myself. Day by day I must learn to abandon myself; to keep myself available for whatever he, the Lord, needs of me at a given moment, even if other things seem more appealing and more important to me: it means giving life, not taking it. It is in this very way that we experience freedom: freedom from ourselves, the vastness of being. In this very way, by being useful, in being a person whom the world needs, our life becomes important and beautiful. Only those who give up their own life find it.

Homily at the ordination of 15 priests (May 7, 2006)

35. To know with the heart

There is no true knowledge without love, without an inner relationship and deep acceptance of the other... His way of knowing his sheep must always also be knowing with the heart.

Homily at the ordination of 15 priests (May 7, 2006)

36. Christian vocation

The first disciples of Jesus... after meeting him by the lake and in the villages of Galilee, were won over by his appeal and his love. The Christian vocation is always a renewal of this personal friendship with Jesus Christ, which gives full meaning to our lives and makes us open to the Kingdom of God.

Regina Caeli (May 7, 2006)

37. The way of God

We too have a desire for God, we too want to be generous, but we too expect God to be strong in the world and to transform the world on the spot, according to our ideas and the needs that we perceive. God chooses a different way. God chooses the way of the transformation of hearts in suffering and in humility.

General audience (May 17, 2006)

38. The priority of God

The fundamental need of the human being, which is the need for God, not for a distant and general God, but for the God who revealed himself in Jesus Christ as love that saves. And it is also possible to shine a new and liberating light on the great problems of the present time. But giving God priority - above all it is we who have need of God - is of great importance.

Address to Italian Episcopal Conference (May 18, 2006)

39. Openness

True knowledge of the love of God is only possible in the context of an attitude of humble prayer and generous availability.

Letter to Company of Jesus (published May 23, 2006)

40. Experience and witness

Faith, because it a fruit of the experience of the love of God is a grace, a gift of God. Man however, may only experience faith as a grace in the measure in which he accepts it within him as a gift by which he seeks to live.

Letter to Company of Jesus (published May 23, 2006)

41. Walking

The school of faith is not a triumphal march but a journey marked daily by suffering and love, trials and faithfulness.

General audience (May 24, 2006)

42. Prayer

Let us not be consumed with haste, as if time dedicated to Christ in silent prayer were time wasted. On the contrary, it is precisely then that the most wonderful fruits … come to birth. There is no need to be discouraged on account of the fact that prayer requires effort, or because of the impression that Jesus remains silent. He is indeed silent, but he is at work.

Address to the Polish clergy (May 25, 2006)

43. Waiting

The faithful expect only one thing from priests: that they be specialists in promoting the encounter between man and God.

Address to the Polish clergy (May 25, 2006)

44. Spiritual fatherhood

We grow in affective maturity when our hearts adhere to God. Christ needs priests who are mature, virile, capable of cultivating an authentic spiritual paternity. For this to happen, priests need to be honest with themselves, open with their spiritual director and trusting in divine mercy.

Address to the Polish clergy (May 25, 2006)

45. Sin

We need to reject the desire to identify only with those who are sinless. How could the Church have excluded sinners from her ranks? It is for their salvation that Jesus took flesh, died and rose again. We must therefore learn to live Christian penance with sincerity. By practicing it, we confess individual sins in union with others, before them and before God.

Address to the Polish clergy (May 25, 2006)

46. The task of faith

Faith does not just mean accepting a certain number of abstract truths about the mysteries of God, of man, of life and death, of future realities. Faith consists in an intimate relationship with Christ, a relationship based on love of him who loved us first (cf. 1 *Jn* 4:11), even to the total offering of himself.

Homily at Piłsudski Square in Warsaw (May 26, 2006)

47. In union with Christ

But what does it mean to love Christ? It means trusting him even in times of trial, following him faithfully even on the Via Crucis, in the hope that soon the morning of the Resurrection will come. Entrusting ourselves to Christ, we lose nothing, we gain everything. In his hands our life acquires its true meaning. Love for Christ expresses itself in the will to harmonise our own life with the thoughts and sentiments of his Heart.

Homily at Piłsudski Square in Warsaw (May 26, 2006)

48. Mystery and faith

God is hidden in mystery; to claim to understand him would mean to want to confine him within our thinking and knowing and consequently to lose him irremediably. With faith, however, we can open up a way through concepts, even theological concepts, and can "touch" the living God. And God, once touched, immediately gives us his power.

Address at the sanctuary of Jasna Góra (May 26, 2006)

49. The way

Faith can always bring us back to God even when our sin leads us astray.

Address at the sanctuary of Jasna Góra (May 26, 2006)

50. Learning Jesus

Mary learned from Jesus! From her very first "fiat", through the long, ordinary years of the hidden life, as she brought up Jesus, or when at Cana in Galilee she asked for the first sign, or when finally on Calvary, by the Cross, she looked on Jesus, she "learned" him moment by moment. Firstly in faith and then in her womb, she received the Body of Jesus and then gave birth to him. Day after day, enraptured, she adored him. She served him with solicitous love, singing the Magnificat in her heart. On your journey of preparation, and in your future priestly ministry, let Mary guide you as you "learn" Jesus. Keep your eyes fixed on him. Let him form you.

Address at the sanctuary of Jasna Góra (May 26, 2006)

51. Leaning on Christ

My friends, do not be afraid to lean on Christ! Long for Christ, as the foundation of your life! Enkindle within you the desire to build your life on him and for him! Because no one who depends on the crucified love of the Incarnate Word can ever lose.

Address to the youth in Krakow (May 27, 2006)

52. Proven faith

A strong faith must endure tests. A living faith must always grow. Our faith in Jesus Christ, to be such, must frequently face others' lack of faith.
Address to the youth in Krakow (May 27, 2006)

53. Believing

To believe means first to accept as true what our mind cannot fully comprehend. We have to accept what God reveals to us about himself, about ourselves, about everything around us, including the things that are invisible, inexpressible and beyond our imagination. This act of accepting revealed truth broadens the horizon of our knowledge and draws us to the mystery in which our lives are immersed. Letting our reason be limited in this way is not something easy to do. Here we see the second aspect of faith: it is trust in a person, no ordinary person, but Jesus Christ himself. What we believe is important, but even more important is the One in whom we believe.
Homily at Błonie Park in Krakow (May 28, 2006)

54. Auschwitz

We cannot peer into God's mysterious plan - we see only piecemeal, and we would be wrong to set ourselves up as judges of God and history. Then we would not be defending man, but only contributing to his downfall. No - when all is said and done, we must

continue to cry out humbly yet insistently to God:
Rouse yourself! Do not forget mankind, your creature!
And our cry to God must also be a cry that pierces
our very heart, a cry that awakens within us God's
hidden presence - so that his power, the power he
has planted in our hearts, will not be buried or
choked within us by the mire of selfishness,
pusillanimity, indifference or opportunism.
Address at Auschwitz (May 28, 2006)

55. Holiness and beauty

Was it not perhaps the beauty born from faith on the
saints' faces that spurred so many men and women
to follow in their footsteps?
Message to World Congress of Ecclesial Movements
(May 31, 2006)

56. The freedom of Christ

There us no valid beauty if there is not a truth to
recognise and follow, if love gives way to transitory
sentiment, if happiness becomes an elusive mirage or
if freedom degenerates into instinct. How much evil
the mania for power, possession and pleasure can
spawn in the lives of people and nations! Take the
witness of the freedom with which Christ set us free
(cf. *Ga* 5:1) to this troubled world.
Message to World Congress of Ecclesial Movements
(May 31, 2006)

57. True faith

Faith as a fundamental attitude of the spirit, is not merely something intellectual or sentimental; true faith involves the entire person: thoughts, affections, intentions, relations, bodylines, activity and daily work.
General audience (May 31, 2006)

June 2006

58. God: the dwelling of man

To love according to God it is necessary to live in him and of him: God is the first "home" of human beings, and only by dwelling in God do men and women burn with a flame of divine love that can set the world "on fire".

Message for the 80th World Mission Day 2006

(June 2, 2006)

59. Freedom and responsibility

True freedom is demonstrated in responsibility, in a way of behaving in which one takes upon oneself a shared responsibility for the world, for oneself and for others... [it is necessary] to look at the world, others and ourselves with God's eyes. We do not do good as slaves who are not free to act otherwise, but we do it because we are personally responsible for the world; because we love truth and goodness, because we love God himself and therefore, also his creatures. This is the true freedom to which the Holy Spirit wants to lead us.

Homily for the Vigil of Pentecost (June 3, 2006)

60. All is gift

Anyone who has come across something true, beautiful and good in his life - the one true treasure, the precious

pearl - hastens to share it everywhere, in the family and at work, in all the contexts of his life. He does so without any fear, because he knows he has received adoption as a son; without any presumption, for it is all a gift.
Homily for the Vigil of Pentecost (June 3, 2006)

61. Thought of by God
The roots of our being and of our action are in the wise and provident silence of God.
Homily for the Solemnity of Pentecost (June 4, 2006)

62. The bridge of the Spirit
Human pride and egoism always create divisions, build walls of indifference, hate and violence. The Holy Spirit, on the other hand, makes hearts capable of understanding the languages of all, as he re-establishes the bridge of authentic communion between earth and heaven.
Homily for the Solemnity of Pentecost (June 4, 2006)

63. Education to faith
Discovering the beauty and joy of faith is a path that every new generation must take on its own, for all that we have that is most our own and most intimate is staked on faith: our heart, our mind, our freedom, in a deeply personal relationship with the Lord at work within us.
Address to Ecclesial Convention of Rome (June 5, 2006)

64. Secularism, agnosticism, relativism

Indeed, it is possible to identify two basic lines of our current secularised society that are clearly interdependent. They impel people to move away from the Christian proclamation and cannot but have an effect on those whose inclinations and choices of life are developing. One of these is agnosticism, which derives from the reduction of human intelligence to a mere practical mechanism that tends to stifle the religious sense engraved in the depths of our nature. The other is the process of relativisation and uprooting, which corrodes the most sacred bonds and most worthy affections of the human being, with the result that people are debilitated and our reciprocal relations rendered precarious and unstable.

Address to Ecclesial Convention of Rome (June 5, 2006)

65. The law of love

Anyone who knows he is loved is in turn prompted to love.

Address to Ecclesial Convention of Rome (June 5, 2006)

66. Marriage

Human love, in fact, needs to be purified, to mature and also to surpass itself if it is to be able to become fully human, to be the beginning of true and lasting joy, to respond, that is, to the question of eternity which it bears within it and which it cannot renounce without betraying itself.

This is the principal reason why love between a man and a woman is only completely fulfilled in marriage.

Address to Ecclesial Convention of Rome (June 5, 2006)

67. The question of truth

By asking the question about the truth, we are in fact broadening the horizon of our rationality, we are beginning to free reason from those excessively narrow boundaries that confine it when we consider as rational only what can be the object of experimentation or calculation. It is here that the encounter between reason and faith takes place. In fact, through faith we accept the gift that God makes of himself in revealing himself to us, creatures made in his image. We welcome and accept that Truth which our minds cannot fully comprehend or possess but which, for this very reason, extends the horizon of our knowledge and enables us to arrive at the Mystery in which we are immersed, and to find in God the definitive meaning of our lives.

Address to Ecclesial Convention of Rome (June 5, 2006)

68. The joy of faith

To the extent that we nourish ourselves on Christ and are in love with him, we feel within us the incentive to bring others to him: indeed, we cannot keep the joy of the faith to ourselves; we must pass it on. This need becomes even stronger and more pressing in the context of that strange forgetfulness of God which has spread in vast areas of the world today ... This forgetfulness is giving rise to a lot of fleeting chatter, to many useless arguments, but also to great dissatisfaction and a sense of emptiness.

Address to Ecclesial Convention of Rome (June 5, 2006)

69. The dynamism of love

All beings are ordered to a dynamic harmony that we can similarly call "love". But only in the human person, who is free and can reason, does this dynamism become spiritual, does it become responsible love, in response to God and to one's neighbour through a sincere gift of self. It is in this love that human beings find their truth and happiness.

Angelus (June 11, 2006)

70. Crosses

Our own crosses acquire value if we consider them and accept them as a part of the Cross of Christ, if a reflection of his light illuminates them. It is by that Cross alone that our sufferings too are ennobled and

acquire their true meaning.
General audience (June 14, 2006)

71. The program for a Christian
Allowing the "I" of Christ to replace our "I".
Angelus (June 25, 2006)

72. "If the Lord wants" (*Jm* 4:15)
[This expression] teaches us not to presume to plan
our lives autonomously and with self interest, but to
make room for the inscrutable will of God, who
knows what is truly good for us.
General audience (June 28, 2006)

73. The path towards the Cross
The Lord is continuously on his way towards the Cross,
towards the lowliness of the servant of God, suffering
and killed, but at the same time he is also on the way
to the immensity of the world in which he precedes us
as the Risen One, so that the light of his words and the
presence of his love may shine forth in the world; he is
on the way so that through him, the Crucified and
Risen Christ, God himself, may arrive in the world.
General audience (June 29, 2006)

74. Christ and the Church
The Church - and in her, Christ - still suffers today. In
her, Christ is again and again taunted and slapped;
again and again an effort is made to reject him from

the world. Again and again the little barque of the Church is ripped apart by the winds of ideologies, whose waters seep into her and seem to condemn her to sink. Yet, precisely in the suffering Church, Christ is victorious. In spite of all, faith in him recovers ever new strength. The Lord also commands the waters today and shows that he is the Lord of the elements. He stays in his barque, in the little boat of the Church.
General audience (June 29, 2006)

75. The prayer of Jesus

The devil - the slanderer of God and men - ... wants to prove that no true religious feeling exists, but that in man every aim is always solely utilitarian ... To us it oftentimes seems that God allows Satan too much freedom, that he grants him the power to distress us too terribly; and that this gets the better of our forces and oppresses us too heavily. Again and again we cry out to God: "Alas, look at the misery of your disciples! Ah, protect us!". In fact, Jesus continues: "I have prayed for you that your faith may not fail" (*Lk* 22:32). Jesus' prayer is the limit set upon the power of the devil.
General audience (June 29, 2006)

76. Jesus' gaze

Jesus' look works the transformation and becomes salvation.
Homily on the feast of Saints Peter and Paul
(June 29, 2006)

July 2006

77. Sequela Christi

The Lord wishes to make each one of us a disciple who lives in personal friendship with him. To achieve this, it is not enough to follow him and to listen to him outwardly: it is also necessary to live with him and like him.

General audience (July 5, 2006)

78. Invitation

Without sufficient recollection it is impossible to approach the supreme mystery of God and of his revelation.

General audience (July 5, 2006)

79. Choice

It is essential that the building of the common European house always be founded on the truth about man, hence, based on the affirmation of each person's right to life, from conception until natural death; on recognition of the spiritual element of the human being in which his inalienable dignity is rooted; and on respect for the religious choices of each person in which his insuppressible openness to the transcendent is witnessed.

Address to the bishops of Croatia (July 6, 2006)

80. The common European home

It is essential that the building of the common European house always be founded on the truth about man, hence, based on the affirmation of each person's right to life, from conception until natural death; on recognition of the spiritual element of the human being in which his inalienable dignity is rooted; and on respect for the religious choices of each person in which his insuppressible openness to the transcendent is witnessed.

Speech to Croatian bishops (July 6, 2006)

81. Forgiveness

Forgiveness above all sets free the person who had the courage to grant it.

Address to the bishops of Croatia (July 6, 2006)

82. Secularism

Prescinding from God, acting as if he did not exist or relegating faith to the purely private sphere, undermines the truth about man and compromises the future of culture and society. On the contrary, lifting one's gaze to the living God, the garantor of our freedom and of truth, is a premise for arriving at a new humanity.

Letter to the bishops of Spain (July 8, 2006)

83. For love

Human beings were created in the image and

likeness of God for love, and that complete human fulfillment only comes about when we make a sincere gift of ourselves to others.

Address at Fifth World Meeting of Families (July 8, 2006)

84. The sacrament of marriage

The family is itself based primarily on a deep interpersonal relationship between husband and wife, sustained by affection and mutual understanding. To enable this, it receives abundant help from God in the sacrament of Matrimony, which brings with it a true vocation to holiness.

Address at Fifth World Meeting of Families (July 8, 2006)

85. The family

None of us gave ourselves life or singlehandedly learned how to live. All of us received from others both life itself and its basic truths, and we have been called to attain perfection in relationship and loving communion with others. The family, founded on indissoluble marriage between a man and a woman, is the expression of this relational, filial and communal aspect of life. It is the setting where men and women are enabled to be born with dignity, and to grow and develop in an integral manner.

Homily at Fifth World Meeting of Families (July 9, 2006)

86. The Christian family

The Christian family passes on the faith when parents teach their children to pray and when they pray with them (cf. *Familiaris Consortio*, 60); when they lead them to the sacraments and gradually introduce them to the life of the Church; when all join in reading the Bible, letting the light of faith shine on their family life and praising God as our Father.

Homily at Fifth World Meeting of Families (July 9, 2006)

87. Christian education

In contemporary culture, we often see an excessive exaltation of the freedom of the individual as an autonomous subject, as if we were self-created and self-sufficient, apart from our relationship with others and our responsibilities in their regard. Attempts are being made to organise the life of society on the basis of subjective and ephemeral desires alone, with no reference to objective, prior truths such as the dignity of each human being and his inalienable rights and duties, which every social group is called to serve. The Church does not cease to remind us that true human freedom derives from our having been created in God's image and likeness. Christian education is consequently an education in freedom and for freedom.

Homily at Fifth World Meeting of Families (July 9, 2006)

88. The disciple

A disciple of Christ is one who, in the experience of human weakness, has had the humility to ask for his help, has been healed by him and has set out following closely after him, becoming a witness of the power of his merciful love that is stronger than sin and death.

Angelus (July 23, 2006)

89. Mystery

We human beings cannot solve the mystery of history, the mystery of the human freedom to say "no" to God's peace. We cannot solve the whole mystery of the God-man relationship, of his action and our response. We must accept the mystery.

Rhêmes-Saint Georges, Aosta Valley (July 23, 2006)

90. The works of God

To recount the works of God is to praise him.

Letter to Cardinal Angelini (July 26, 2006)

August 2006

91. A bottled up world

It has become more difficult to believe because the world in which we find ourselves is completely made up of ourselves, and God, so to speak, does not appear directly anymore. We do not drink from the source anymore, but from the vessel which is offered to us already full, and so on. Humanity has rebuilt the world by itself, and finding God inside this world has become more difficult.

Vatican Radio interview (August 5, 2006)

92. To young people

[Have the] courage to make definitive decisions!... they are really the only ones that allow us to grow, to move ahead and to reach something great in life. They are the only decisions that do not destroy our freedom but offer to point us in the right direction. Risk making this leap, so to speak, towards the definitive and so embrace life fully: this is something I would be happy to communicate to them.

Vatican Radio interview (August 5, 2006)

93. Positive option

Christianity, Catholicism, is not a collection of prohibitions: it is a positive option. It is very important that we look at it again because this idea has almost completely disappeared today.

Vatican Radio interview (August 5, 2006)

94. True progress

Progress becomes true progress only if it serves the human person and if the human person grows: not only in terms of his or her technical power, but also in his or her moral awareness.

Vatican Radio interview (August 5, 2006)

95. The formation of the heart

I believe that the real problem of our historical moment lies in the imbalance between the incredibly fast growth of our technical power and that of our moral capacity, which has not grown in proportion.... We need two dimensions: simultaneously, we need the formation of the heart, if I can express myself in this way, with which the human person acquires points of reference and learns how to use the techniques correctly.

Vatican Radio interview (August 5, 2006)

96. God, reason and culture

That's why we must, and we can, show that, precisely because of the new intercultural environment in which we live, pure rationality separated from God is insufficient. We need a wider rationality that sees God in harmony with reason and is aware that the Christian faith that developed in Europe is also a means to bring together reason and culture and to integrate them with action in a single and comprehensive vision.

Vatican Radio Interview (August 5, 2006)

97. Women in the Church

I believe that women themselves, with their energy and strength, with their predominance, so to speak, with what I would call their "spiritual power", will know how to make their own space. And we will have to try and listen to God so as not to oppose him but, on the contrary, to rejoice when the female element achieves the fully effective place in the Church best suited to it, starting with the Mother of God and with Mary Magdalene.

Vatican Radio interview (August 5, 2006)

98. Lightness of spirit

A writer once said that angels can fly because they do not take themselves too seriously. Maybe we could also fly a bit if we did not think we were so important.

Vatican Radio interview (August 5, 2006)

99. Holidays

For many, vacation time becomes a profitable occasion for cultural contacts, for prolonged moments of prayer and of contemplation in contact with nature or in monasteries and religious structures. Having more free time, one can dedicate oneself more easily to conversation with God, meditation on Sacred Scripture and reading some useful, formative book. Those who experience this spiritual repose know how useful it is not to reduce vacations to mere relaxation and amusement.

Angelus (August 13, 2006)

100. The Saints of God

We do not praise God sufficiently by keeping silent about his saints.

Homily on the Assumption of Mary (August 15, 2006)

101. With God

If God does not exist, life is empty, the future is empty. And if God exists, everything changes, life is light, our future is light and we have guidance for how to live.

Homily on the Assumption of Mary (August 15, 2006)

102. Believing

To believe is not only a way of thinking or an idea; as has already been mentioned, it is a way of acting, a manner of living.

Homily on the Assumption of Mary (August 15, 2006)

103. Fear of God

"Fear of God" is not anguish; it is something quite different... Fear of God is that sense of responsibility that we are bound to possess, responsibility for the portion of the world that has been entrusted to us in our lives.

Homily on the Assumption of Mary (August 15, 2006)

104. Already but not yet

Some people today live as if they never had to die or as if, with death, everything were over; others, who hold that man is the one and only author of his own destiny, behave as though God did not exist, and at times they even reach the point of denying that there is room for him in our world. Yet, the great breakthroughs of technology and science that have considerably improved humanity's condition leave unresolved the deepest searchings of the human soul. Only openness to the mystery of God, who is Love, can quench the thirst for truth and happiness in our hearts; only the prospect of eternity can give authentic value to historical events and especially to the mystery of human frailty, suffering and death.

General audience (August 16, 2006)

105. The sense of activism

It is necessary, the Saint observes, to beware of the dangers of excessive activity whatever one's condition and office, because, as he said to the Pope of that time and to all Popes, to all of us, many occupations frequently lead to "hardness of heart", "they are none other than suffering of spirit, loss of understanding, dispersion of grace" (Saint Bernard). This warning applies to every kind of occupation, even those inherent in the government of the Church.

Angelus (August 20, 2006)

106. Mother Church

The Church, the People of God of all times, the Church in all ages, with great suffering, brings forth Christ ever anew.

General audience (August 23, 2006)

107. Grace

The good news of the Gospel consists precisely in this: offering God's grace to the sinner!

General audience (August 30, 2006)

108. Explanation

"Faith": that is, a relationship with God, acquaintanceship with God.

To priests of the Diocese of Albano (August 31, 2006)

109. *Ars celebrandi*

It is important, therefore, to enter into this conversation. St Benedict in his "Rule" tells the monks, speaking of the recitation of the Psalms,

"*Mens concordet voci*". The vox, words, precede our mind. This is not usually the case: one has to think first, then one's thought becomes words. But here, the words come first. The sacred Liturgy gives us the words; we must enter into these words, find a harmony with this reality that precedes us.

To priests of the Diocese of Albano (August 31, 2006)

110. Crisis

We must learn the need for suffering and for crises. We must put up with and transcend this suffering. Only in this way is life enriched. I believe that the fact the Lord bears the stigmata for eternity has a symbolic value. As an expression of the atrocity of suffering and death, today the stigmata are seals of Christ's victory, of the full beauty of his victory and his love for us.

To priests of the Diocese of Albano (August 31, 2006)

111. Conversion

[Conversion is] the joy that God exists and is concerned about us, that we have access to God and can help others "rebuild his House".

To priests of the Diocese of Albano (August 31, 2006)

September 2006

112. The pedagogy of peace

First of all peace must be built in hearts. It is here, in fact, that sentiments develop that can nurture it or, on the contrary, threaten, weaken and stifle it. Moreover, the human heart is the place where God intervenes.
Message to Bishop of Assisi-Nocera (September 2, 2006)

113. Friend

What is important is to "learn Christ" (4:20): therefore, not only and not so much to listen to his teachings and words as rather to know him in person, that is, his humanity and his divinity, his mystery and his beauty. In fact, he is not only a Teacher but a Friend, indeed, a Brother. How will we be able to get to know him properly by being distant? Closeness, familiarity and habit make us discover the true identity of Jesus Christ.
General audience (September 6, 2006)

114. The fathers of the Chruch

The Fathers were speaking to and about the men and women of their time. But their message also has new meaning for us modern men and women.
Homily at Neue Messe, Munich (September 10, 2006)

115. Respect

The tolerance which we urgently need includes the fear of God - respect for what others hold sacred. This respect for what others hold sacred demands that we ourselves learn once more the fear of God. But this sense of respect can be reborn in the Western world only if faith in God is reborn, if God become once more present to us and in us.

Homily at Neue Messe, Munich (September 10, 2006)

116. *Ancilla Domini*

[Mary] is and remains the handmaid of the Lord who does not put herself at the centre, but wants to lead us towards God, to teach us a way of life in which God is acknowledge as the centre of all there is and the centre of our personal lives.

Angelus (September 10, 2006)

117. "And he dwelt amongst us" (*Jn* 1:14)

God is not far from us, he is not somewhere out in the universe, somewhere that none of us can go. He has pitched his tent among us: in Jesus he became one of us, flesh and blood just like us. This is his "tent"... In Jesus, it is God who "camps" in our midst.

Homily at the Cathedral of Munich (September 10, 2006)

118. Answers

Any answers that do not finally lead to God are insufficient.

Homily at the Cathedral of Munich (September 10, 2006)

119. The call

Mary received her vocation from the lips of an angel. The Angel does not enter our room visibly, but the Lord has a plan for each of us, he calls each one of us by name. Our task is to learn how to listen, to perceive his call, to be courageous and faithful in following him and, when all is said and done, to be found trustworthy servants who have used well the gifts given us.

Homily, Vespers at St Anne's Basilica, Altötting
(September 12, 2006)

120. Witnesses

To be a witness of Jesus Christ means above all to bear witness to a certain way of living. In a world full of confusion we must again bear witness to the standards that make life truly life.

Homily at Regensburg Cathedral (September 12, 2006)

121. The spirit of the liturgy

The more we allow ourselves, through the liturgy, to be transformed in Christ, the more we will be capable of transforming the world, radiating Christ's goodness, his mercy and his love for others.

Greeting, Regensburg's Alte Kapelle (September 13, 2006)

122. Prudence

Prudence will make you patient with yourselves and with others, courageous and firm in your decisions, merciful and just, concerned solely with your salvation and the salvation of your brethren "with fear and trembling" (cf. Ph 2: 12).

Address to recently appointed Bishops

(September 21, 2006)

123. Explanations

[Let us have the courage] to ask Jesus for explanations. We often do not understand him. Let us be brave enough to say: "I do not understand you, Lord; listen to me, help me to understand". In such a way, with this frankness which is the true way of praying, of speaking to Jesus, we express our meagre capacity to understand and at the same time place ourselves in the trusting attitude of someone who expects light and strength from the One able to provide them.

General audience (September 27, 2006)

October 2006

124. The extraordinariness of the ordinary

Attachment to Jesus can also be lived and witnessed to without performing sensational deeds. Jesus himself, to whom each one of us is called to dedicate his or her own life and death, is and remains extraordinary.

General audience (October 4, 2006)

125. Silence and contemplation

Silence and contemplation have a purpose: they serve, in the distractions of daily life, to preserve permanent union with God. This is their purpose: that union with God may always be present in our souls and may transform our entire being.

Homily, Theological Commission (October 6, 2006)

126. Subject

God, in reality, is not the object but the subject of theology. The one who speaks through theology, the speaking subject, must be God himself. And our Address and thoughts must always serve to ensure that what God says, the Word of God, is listened to and finds room in the world.

Homily, Theological Commission (October 6, 2006)

127. Bearers of the truth

I think that this is the fundamental virtue for the theologian, this discipline of obedience to the truth,

which makes us, although it may be hard, collaborators of the truth, mouthpieces of truth, for it is not we who speak in today's river of words, but it is the truth which speaks in us, who are really purified and made chaste by obedience to the truth. So it is that we can truly be harbingers of the truth.
Homily, Theological Commission (October 6, 2006)

128. The sense of sin

Where God is excluded from the public forum the sense of offence against God - the true sense of sin - dissipates, just as when the absolute value of moral norms is relativised the categories of good or evil vanish, along with individual responsibility.
Address to Bishops, Western Canada (October 9, 2006)

129. With an open heart

The Risen One must be seen, must be perceived also by the heart, in a way so that God may take up his abode within us. The Lord does not appear as a thing. He desires to enter our lives, and therefore his manifestation is a manifestation that implies and presupposes an open heart. Only in this way do we see the Risen One.
General audience (October 11, 2006)

130. Couplet

Prayer and charity, God and neighbour. The Gospel does not allow short cuts. Whoever addresses the

God of Jesus Christ is spurred to serve the brethren; and vice versa, whoever dedicates himself or herself to the poor, discovers there the mysterious Face of God.

Address, Charitable Works of Padre Pio of Pietrelcina
(October 14, 2006)

131. Law and grace

To "enter into life" it is necessary to observe the commandments (cf. *Mk* 10:19). It is necessary, but not sufficient! In fact, as St Paul says, salvation does not come from the law, but from Grace. And St John recalls that the law was given by Moses, while Grace and Truth come by means of Jesus Christ (cf. *Jn* 1:17). To reach salvation one must therefore be open in faith to the grace of Christ.

Homily, canonisation of 4 Servants of God
(October 15, 2006)

132. Anchor

Christian hope is rooted in a solid faith and the word of God. It is the anchor of salvation that aids us in overcoming those difficulties that appear insurmountable, and allows us to peer at the light of joy even beyond the darkness of pain and death.

Homily for Funeral of Cardinal Dino Monduzzi
(October 16, 2006)

133. Point of view

The possibilities to pervert the human heart are truly many. The only way to prevent it consists in not cultivating an individualistic, autonomous vision of things, but on the contrary, by putting oneself always on the side of Jesus, assuming his point of view. We must daily seek to build full communion with him.

General audience (October 18, 2006)

134. "Never despair of the Divine Mercy" (Saint Bernard)

God "is greater than our hearts", as St John says (I *Jn* 3:20). Let us remember two things. The first: Jesus respects our freedom. The second: Jesus awaits our openness to repentance and conversion; he is rich in mercy and forgiveness.

General audience (October 18, 2006)

135. Secularism

The culture that predominates in the West and seeks to present itself as universal and self-sufficient, [generates] a new custom of life. From this a new wave of enlightenment and laicism is derived, by which only what is experiential and calculable would be rationally valid, while on the level of praxis, individual freedom is held as a fundamental value to which all others must be subject. Therefore, God remains excluded from culture and from public life, and faith in him becomes more difficult, also because we live in a world that almost always appears to be of our making, in which, so to speak, God no longer appears directly but seems to have become superfluous, even out of place.

Address to the Fourth National Ecclesial Convention
(October 19, 2006)

136. The person

The human person is not only reason and intelligence, although they are constitutive elements. He bears within himself, written in the most profound depths of his being, the need for love, to be loved and in turn to love. Therefore, he questions himself and often feels lost before the harshness of life, the evil that exists in the world and that appears so strong and at the same time radically devoid of sense. Particularly in our age, notwithstanding all the progress made, evil has certainly not been overcome. Indeed, its power seems reinforced and all the attempts to hide it are quickly unveiled, as both daily experience and great historical events demonstrate.

Address to the Fourth National Ecclesial Convention
(October 19, 2006)

137. The cross

Rightly, the Cross causes us fear, as it provoked fear and anguish in Jesus Christ (cf. *Mk* 14:33-36); but it is not a negation of life, of which in order to be happy it is necessary to rid oneself. It is rather the extreme "yes" of God to man, the supreme expression of his love and the source of full and perfect life. It therefore contains the most convincing invitation to follow Christ on the way of gift of self.

Address to the Fourth National Ecclesial Convention
(October 19, 2006)

138. Education

A true education must awaken the courage to make definitive decisions, which today are considered a mortifying bind to our freedom. In reality, they are indispensable for growth and in order to achieve something great in life, in particular, to cause love to mature in all its beauty: therefore, to give consistency and meaning to freedom itself.

Address to the Fourth National Ecclesial Convention
(October 19, 2006)

139. Evangelisation

To do this, we must return to proclaiming powerfully and joyfully the event of Christ's death and Resurrection, heart of Christianity, principal fulcrum of our faith, powerful lever of our certainty, impetuous

wind that sweeps away every fear and indecision, every doubt and human calculation. This decisive change in the world can only come from God.
Homily, National Ecclesial Convention

(October 19, 2006)

140. Evangelisation

In a changing world, the Gospel does not alter. The Good News always remains the same: Christ has died and is risen for our salvation! In his Name take the message of conversion and forgiveness for sins to everyone, but be yourselves the first to witness to a converted and forgiven life.
Homily, National Ecclesial Convention

(October 19, 2006)

141. "Behold your mother" (*Jn* 19:27)

One must remain in prayer with Mary, the Mother given to us by Christ from the Cross.
Homily, National Ecclesial Convention

(October 19, 2006)

142. Doing and being

The contemporary context seems to give primacy to an artificial intelligence that becomes ever more dominated by experimental techniques, and in this way forgets that all science must always safeguard man and promote his aspiration for the authentic good. To overrate "doing", obscuring "being", does not help to recompose the fundamental balance that everyone needs in order to give their own existence a solid foundation and valid goal.

Address to the Pontifical Lateran University

(October 21, 2006)

143. Before the crucifix

When one stops to pray before a Crucifix with his glance fixed on that pierced side, he cannot but experience within himself the joy of knowing that he is loved and the desire to love and to make himself an instrument of mercy and reconciliation.

Angelus (October 22, 2006)

144. Intimacy

Whoever wants to be a friend of Jesus and become his authentic disciple - be it seminarian, priest, Religious or lay person - must cultivate an intimate friendship with him in meditation and prayer.

Address to the Pontifical Universities of Rome

(October 23, 2006)

145. Education to silence

One must become capable of listening to God speaking in the heart ... Only if they are born from the silence of contemplation can our words have some value and usefulness, and not resemble the

inflated discourses of the world that seek the consensus of public opinion.
Address to the Pontifical Universities of Rome
(October 23, 2006)

146. Christ-centeredness

What counts is to place Jesus Christ at the centre of our lives, so that our identity is marked essentially by the encounter, by communion with Christ and with his Word. In his light every other value is recovered and purified from possible dross.
General audience (October 25, 2006)

147. Etymology

Gospel - literally, "good news" - known, to announce the grace destined to reconcile men with God, self and others.
General audience (October 25, 2006)

148. Mission and evangelization

The Church is missionary by nature and her principal task is evangelization, which aims to proclaim and to witness to Christ and to promote his Gospel of peace and love in every environment and culture.
Address to the International Congress of Military Ordinariates (October 26, 2006)

149. The path of enlightenment

Faith is a journey of illumination: it starts with the humility of recognising oneself as needy of salvation and arrives at the personal encounter with Christ, who calls one to follow him on the way of love.

Angelus (October 29, 2006)

November 2006

150. Holiness

Being a Saint means living close to God, to live in his family.
Homily for the Mass of All Saints (November 1, 2006)

151. The way of the cross

The Church's experience shows that every form of holiness, even if it follows different paths, always passes through the Way of the Cross, the way of self-denial. The Saints' biographies describe men and women who, docile to the divine plan, sometimes faced unspeakable trials and suffering, persecution and martyrdom.
Homily for the Mass of All Saints (November 1, 2006)

152. To love

Loving always entails an act of self-denial, "losing ourselves", and it is precisely this that makes us happy.
Homily for the Mass of All Saints (November 1, 2006)

153. The man of the beatitudes

The Beatitudes show us the spiritual features of Jesus.
Homily for the Mass of All Saints (November 1, 2006)

154. "Nothing is impossible to God" (cfr. *Lk* 1:37)

With [Jesus] the impossible becomes possible and even a camel can pass through the eye of a needle (cf. *Mk* 10:25); with his help, only with his help, can we become

perfect as the Heavenly Father is perfect (cf. *Mt* 5:48).
Homily for the Mass of All Saints (November 1, 2006)

155. The need for transcendence

In our time more than in the past, people are so
absorbed by earthly things that at times they find it
difficult to think about God as the protagonist of
history and of our own existence. By its nature,
however, human life reaches out for something
greater which transcends it; the human yearning for
justice, truth and full happiness is irrepressible.
Angelus (November 1, 2006)

156. To love in order to know

However, knowing God is not enough. For a true
encounter with him one must also love him.
Knowledge must become love.
Address to the Pontifical Gregorian University

(November 3, 2006)

157. The answer to secularism

Man, both in his interiority and in his exteriority,
cannot be fully understood unless he recognises that
he is open to transcendence. Deprived of his
reference to God, man cannot respond to the
fundamental questions that trouble and will always
trouble his heart concerning the end of his life,
hence, also its meaning... Human destiny without

reference to God cannot but be the desolation of anguish, which leads to desperation. Only in reference to God's Love which is revealed in Jesus Christ can man find the meaning of his existence and live in hope, even if he must face evils that injure his personal existence and the society in which he lives.

Address to the Pontifical Gregorian University
(November 3, 2006)

158. The virtue of hope

Hope ensures that man does not withdraw into a paralysing and sterile nihilism but opens himself instead to generous commitment within the society where he lives in order to improve it. This is the task that God entrusted to man when he created him in his own image and likeness, a task that fills every human being with the greatest possible dignity, but also with an immense responsibility.

Address to the Pontifical Gregorian University
(November 3, 2006)

159. Science and revelation

Man cannot place in science and technology so radical and unconditional a trust as to believe that scientific and technological progress can explain everything and completely fulfill all his existential and spiritual needs. Science cannot replace philosophy and revelation by giving an exhaustive answer to man's most radical questions: questions about the meaning of living and dying, about ultimate values, and about the nature of progress itself.

Address to the Pontifical Academy of Sciences

(November 6, 2006)

160. Freedom and history

Only humanity, strictly speaking, has a history, the history of its freedom. Freedom, like reason, is a precious part of God's image within us, and it can never be reduced to a deterministic analysis. Its transcendence vis-à-vis the material world must be acknowledged and respected, since it is a sign of our human dignity.

Address to the Pontifical Academy of Sciences

(November 6, 2006

161. The sense of God

When man is entirely caught up in his own world, with material things, with what he can do, with all that is feasible and brings him success, with all that he can produce or understand by himself, then his capacity to perceive God weakens, the organ sensitive to God deteriorates, it becomes unable to perceive and sense, it no longer perceives the Divine, because the corresponding inner organ has withered, it has stopped developing. When he overuses all the other organs, the empirical ones, it can happen that it is precisely the sense of God that suffers, that this organ

dies, and man, as St Gregory says, no longer perceives God's gaze, to be looked at by him, the fact that his precious gaze touches me! when man is entirely caught up in his own world, with material things, with what he can do, with all that is feasible and brings him success, with all that he can produce or understand by himself, then his capacity to perceive God weakens, the organ sensitive to God deteriorates, it becomes unable to perceive and sense, it no longer perceives the Divine, because the corresponding inner organ has withered, it has stopped developing. When he overuses all the other organs, the empirical ones, it can happen that it is precisely the sense of God that suffers, that this organ dies, and man, as St Gregory says, no longer perceives God's gaze, to be looked at by him, the fact that his precious gaze touches me!
Homily to the Swiss Bishops (November 7, 2006)

162. Thinking with the heart

Learn to think as Christ thought, learn to think with him! And this thinking is not only the thinking of the mind, but also a thinking of the heart. We learn Jesus Christ's sentiments when we learn to think with him
Homily to the Swiss Bishops (November 7, 2006)

163. "Your faith has healed you"

"*Fides tua te salvum fecit*", the Lord said over and over again to those he healed. It was not the physical touch, it was not the external gesture that was operative, but the fact that those sick people believed. And we too can only serve the Lord energetically if our faith thrives and is present in abundance.

Address to the Swiss Bishops (November 7, 2006)

164. Forgiveness

The widespread absence of an awareness of sin is a disturbing phenomenon of our time. Thus, the gift of the Sacrament of Penance not only consists in the reception of forgiveness, but also and above all in being aware of our need for forgiveness. With this Sacrament we are purified, we are inwardly transformed and subsequently able to understand others even better and to forgive them.

Address to the Swiss Bishops (November 7, 2006)

165. Identity

Christian identity is composed of precisely two elements: this restraint from seeking oneself by oneself but instead receiving oneself from Christ and giving oneself with Christ, thereby participating personally in the life of Christ himself to the point of identifying with him and sharing both his death and his life.

General audience (November 8, 2006)

166. Greatness

Let us return, therefore, to the subject of "God". The words of St Ignatius spring to mind: "The Christian is

not the result of persuasion, but of power (*Epistula ad Romanos* 3, 3). We should not allow our faith to be drained by too many discussions of multiple, minor details, but rather, should always keep our eyes in the first place on the greatness of Christianity.
Address to the Swiss Bishops (November 9, 2006)

167. To pray is to hope
Prayer is hope in action. And in fact, true reason is contained in prayer, which is why it is possible to hope: we can come into contact with the Lord of the world, he listens to us, and we can listen to him.
Address to the Swiss Bishops (November 9, 2006)

168. Faith and reason
Faith can offer perspectives of hope to every project that has human destiny at its core. Faith examines the invisible and is thus a friend of reason, which asks itself the essential questions from which it draws meaning for our earthly journey.
Address to "Sacred Family of Nazareth Foundation"
(November 11, 2006)

169. Immigrants
In this misfortune experienced by the Family of Nazareth, obliged to take refuge in Egypt, we can catch a glimpse of the painful condition in which all migrants live, especially, refugees, exiles, evacuees,

internally displaced persons, those who are persecuted. We can take a quick look at the difficulties that every migrant family lives through, the hardships and humiliations, the deprivation and fragility of millions and millions of migrants, refugees and internally displaced people. The Family of Nazareth reflects the image of God safeguarded in the heart of every human family, even if disfigured and weakened by emigration.

Message for World Day of Migrants and Refugees
(November 14, 2006)

170. Sons of God

"You did not receive the spirit of slavery to fall back into fear, but you have received the spirit of sonship. When we cry, "Abba! Father!', it is the Spirit himself" (*Rm* 8:2, 15) who speaks in us because, as children, we can call God "Father" … This is our greatest dignity: to be not merely images but also children of God.

General audience (November 15, 2006)

171. Ecumenical dialogue

What should be encouraged first of all is the ecumenism of love, which directly descends from the new commandment that Jesus left to his disciples. Love accompanied by consistent behaviour creates trust and opens hearts and eyes. The dialogue of charity nourishes and enlightens by its nature the dialogue of truth: indeed, the definitive encounter to which the Spirit of Christ leads us will take place in the full truth.

Address to the Pontifical Council for Promoting Christian Unity (November 17, 2006)

172. Proclamation

The first point is the proclamation of the faith to the youth of our time. Young people today live in a secularised culture, totally oriented to material things. In daily life - in the means of communication, at work, in leisure time - they experience at most a culture in which God is absent. Yet, they are waiting for God.

Address to Bishops of Germany (November 18, 2006)

173. "Yes"

Love reaches its true maturity in the patience required by being together for the whole of life.

Address to Bishops of Germany (November 18, 2006)

174. Serving harmony

Playing together as soloists not only requires the individual to make the most of all his technical and musical skills in playing his own part, but at the same time, he must also know how to stand back to listen attentively to others. Only if the soloist succeeds in doing this, that is, if no one monopolises centre stage but in a spirit of service fits in with the whole group and as it were makes himself available as an "instrument" ... This is also a beautiful image for us who, in the context of the Church, are committed to being "instruments" in order to communicate to people the thought of the great "Composer", whose work is the harmony of the universe.

Address at Concert in honour of the Holy Father

(November 18, 2006)

175. Church

History shows us that one usually reaches Jesus by passing through the Church!

General audience (November 22, 2006)

176. Body of Christ

In the same Eucharist, Christ gives us his Body and makes us his Body.

General audience (November 22, 2006)

177. Christians

This is our definition: we belong among those who call on the Name of the Lord Jesus Christ.

General audience (November 22, 2006)

178. Truth and love

Neither Love nor Truth are ever imposed: they come knocking at the doors of the heart and the mind and

where they can enter they bring peace and joy.
Angelus (November 26, 2006)

179. Common itinerary

[We Christians and Muslims] can offer a credible response to the question which emerges clearly from today's society, even if it is often brushed aside, the question about the meaning and purpose of life, for each individual and for humanity as a whole. We are called to work together, so as to help society to open itself to the transcendent, giving Almighty God his rightful place.
Address to the Religious Affairs Directorate
(November 29, 2006)

180. The lesson of the fathers

The Greek Fathers have left us a store of treasure from which the Church continues to draw riches old and new (cf. *Mt* 13:52).
Address on the Feast of Saint Andrew the Apostle
(November 30, 2006)

December 2006

181. Beatitude

We are blessed when the Holy Spirit opens for us the joy of believing.

Homily at the Cathedral of the Holy Spirit in Istanbul

(December 1, 2006)

182. Mission

The Church's mission is not to preserve power, or to gain wealth; her mission is to offer Christ, to give a share in Christ's own life, man's most precious good, which God himself gives us in his Son.

Homily at the Cathedral of the Holy Spirit in Istanbul

(December 1, 2006)

183. Spiritual advent

"In the first [coming]", St Bernard wrote, "Christ was our redemption; in the last coming he will reveal himself to us as our life: in this lies our repose and consolation" (*Discourse 5 on Advent*, 1). The archetype for that coming of Christ, which we might call a "spiritual incarnation", is always Mary. Just as the Virgin Mother pondered in her heart on the Word made flesh, so every individual soul and the entire Church are called during their earthly pilgrimage to wait for Christ who comes and to welcome him with faith and love ever new.

Homily, First Vespers, 1st Sunday of Advent

(December 2, 2006)

184. Peace

For believers "peace" is one of the most beautiful names of God.

Homily, First Vespers, 1st Sunday of Advent
(December 2, 2006)

185. Task

The primary task of evangelisation is to show the savior of every man in Jesus Christ. Never tire of entrusting yourselves to him and proclaiming him with your life, at home and in every environment. Even today, this is what men are waiting for from the Church, from Christians.

Greeting pilgrims of Lazio, Italy (December 6, 2006)

186. To generate Christ

[Mary] welcomed Jesus with faith and gave him to the world with love. This is also our vocation and our mission, the vocation and mission of the Church: to welcome Christ into our lives and give him to the world, so 'that the world might be saved through him' (*Jn* 3:17).

Angelus (December 8, 2006)

187. True justice

True justice cannot be invented by man: rather, it has to be discovered. In other words, it must come from God, who is justice.

Homily at visit to Our Lady Star of Evangelisation Parish (December 10, 2006)

188. The feast of gifts

Christmas is the day when God gave a great gift to us, not something material, but his gift was the gift of himself. He gave us his Son, so Christmas became the feast of gifts.

Greeting to Our Lady Star of Evangelisation Parish

(December 10, 2006)

189. Advent

Thus, to prepare oneself for Christmas means to be committed to building the "dwelling of God with men". No one is excluded; everyone can and must contribute in order to make this house of communion more spacious and beautiful.

Angelus (December 10, 2006)

190. In the heart

Notwithstanding many forms of progress human beings have remained what they have always been: a freedom kept in tension between good and evil, between life and death. It is there, in his intimate recesses, what the bible calls "the heart", that he is always in need of "salvation".

Christmas message (December 25, 2006)

January 2007

191. Wish

Let us begin this new year, therefore, by looking at Mary whom we received from God's hands as a precious "talent" to be made fruitful, a providential opportunity to contribute to bringing about the Kingdom of God.

Homily, Solemnity of Mary (January 1, 2007)

192. Goal

"To listen" to Jesus: to believe in him and gently follow him, doing his will. In this way everyone can tend to holiness, a goal that constitutes the vocation of all the baptised.

Angelus (January 7, 2007)

193. For man

It is by respecting the human person that peace can be promoted, and it is by building peace that the foundations of an authentic integral humanism are laid. This is where I find the answer to the concern for the future voiced by so many of our contemporaries.

Address to the Diplomatic Corps (January 8, 2007)

194. Witness

The value of witness is irreplaceable, because the Gospel leads to it and the Church is nourished by it.

General audience (January 10, 2007)

195. Road

The cross is the path on which Christ comes among us ever anew.

General audience (January 10, 2007)

196. Service

Any relief to the suffering of their neighbour which Christians offer together, however little, also helps to make more visible their communion and fidelity to the Lord's command.

General audience (January 17, 2007)

197. Dialogue

Christ can do all things, "he makes the deaf hear and the mute speak" (*Mk* 7:37). He is capable of imbuing Christians with the ardent desire to listen to the other, to communicate with the other and, together with him, speak the language of reciprocal love.

Angelus (January 21, 2007)

198. The saints

Holiness increases the capacity for conversion, for repentance, for willingness to start again and, especially, for reconciliation and forgiveness... Consequently, it is not the fact that we have never erred but our capacity for reconciliation and forgiveness which makes us saints. And we can all learn this way of holiness.

General audience (January 31, 2007)

February 2007

199. To consecrated people

May you feel challenged by every suffering, every injustice and every search for truth, beauty and goodness. This is not because you can come up with the solution to all problems; rather, it is because every circumstance in which human beings live and die is an opportunity for you to witness to God's saving work. This is your mission.

Address to the Symposium of Secular Institutes
(February 3, 2007)

200. To young people

May the Holy Spirit make you creative in charity, persevering in your commitments, and brave in your initiatives, so that you will be able to offer your contribution to the building up of the "civilisation of love". The horizon of love is truly boundless: it is the whole world!

Message for the XXII WYD (February 5, 2007)

201. Domestic Church

Every home can transform itself in a little church. Not only in the sense that in them must reign the typical Christian love made of altruism and of reciprocal care, but still more in the sense that the whole of family life, based on faith, is called to revolve around

the singular lordship of Jesus Christ.
General audience (February 7, 2007)

202. Proximity

For the Christian, man, however distant, is never a stranger.
Address to Bishop-friends of the Focolare Movement and the Community of St. Egidio (February 8, 2007)

203. Witness

Every baptised person must "live the Gospel".
Address to Misericordie d'Italia (February 10, 2007)

204. The courage of the truth

One of the challenges for our contemporaries, and in particular for youth, consists in not accepting to live merely in exteriority, in appearance, but in the development of the interior life, the unifying environment of being and acting, the place of recognising our dignity as sons and daughters of God called to freedom, not separating ourselves from the font of life but remaining connected to it.
Address to Academy of Moral and Political Sciences, Paris (February 10, 2007)

205. Appearance and reality

One of the challenges for our contemporaries, and in particular for youth, consists in not accepting to live merely in exteriority, in appearance, but in the development of the interior life, the unifying environment of being and acting, the place of recognizing our dignity as sons and daughters of God called to freedom, not separating ourselves from the font of life but remaining connected to it.

Address to Academy of Moral and Political Sciences (February 10, 2007)

206. Gladness

What gladdens man's heart is the recognition of being a son or daughter of God; it is a beautiful and good life under the gaze of God, as are also the victories obtained over evil and against deceit.

Address to Academy of Moral and Political Sciences, Paris (February 10, 2007)

207. Ethics and science

Not all that is scientifically possible is also ethically licit.

Address to Congress on Natural Moral Law sponsored by Pontifical Lateran University (February 12, 2007)

208. Feminine genius

In short, without the generous contribution of many women, the history of Christianity would have developed very differently.

General audience (February 14, 2007)

209. Grace

It is good to recognise one's weakness because in this way we know that we stand in need of the Lord's grace.

Address, Pontifical Major Seminary (February 17, 2007)

210. Way

The journey after conversion is still a journey of conversion.

Address, Pontifical Major Seminary (February 17, 2007)

211. In the love of God

The true treasure of our life is living in the Lord's love and never losing this love.

Address, Pontifical Major Seminary (February 17, 2007)

212. Following

It is precisely in walking with the Lord's Cross that the journey will bear fruit.

Address, Pontifical Major Seminary (February 17, 2007)

213. Conversion

To convert is to seek God.

General audience (February 21, 2007)

214. Happiness

God is love, and his love is the secret of our happiness.

General audience (February 21, 2007)

215. Personal prayer

Let us learn from Mary and speak personally with the Lord, pondering and preserving God's words in our lives and hearts so that they may become true food for each one of us. Thus, Mary guides us at a school of prayer in personal and profound contact with God.
Meeting for Clergy of Rome Diocese (February 22, 2007)

216. For others

True contemplation is expressed in works of charity ... we have experienced in the encounter with Christ, that we exist "for others"".
Meeting for Clergy of Rome Diocese (February 22, 2007)

217. The Face of God

Only if we manage to grasp that Jesus is not a great prophet or a world religious figure but that he is the Face of God, that he is God, have we discovered Christ's greatness and found out who God is. God is not only a distant shadow, the "primary Cause", but he has a Face. His is the Face of mercy, the Face of pardon and love, the Face of the encounter with us.
Meeting for Clergy of Rome Diocese (February 22, 2007)

218. Scripture

The whole Book is a process of constantly new interpretations where one enters ever more deeply into the mystery proposed at the beginning, and that what

was initially present but still closed, unfolds increasingly.
Meeting for Clergy of Rome Diocese (February 22, 2007)

219. The Word

The Word is always far greater than what you have been able to understand.
Meeting for Clergy of Rome Diocese (February 22, 2007)

220. Charisms

Do not extinguish charisms. If the Lord gives us new gifts we must be grateful, even if at times they may be inconvenient. And it is beautiful that without an initiative of the hierarchy but with an initiative from below, as people say, but which also truly comes from on High, that is, as a gift of the Holy Spirit, new forms of life are being born in the Church just as, moreover, they were born down the ages.
Meeting for Clergy of Rome Diocese (February 22, 2007)

221. The priest

[The priest] is a man of prayer, a man of forgiveness, a man who receives and celebrates the sacraments as acts of prayer and encounter with the Lord. He is a man of charity, lived and practised, thus all the simple acts, conversation, encounter, everything that needs to be done, become spiritual acts in communion with Christ. His "*pro omnibus*" becomes our "*pro meis*".
Meeting for Clergy of Rome Diocese (February 22, 2007)

222. The homily

If the homily is developed from prayer, from listening to the Word of God; it is a communication of the content of the Word of God.

Meeting for Clergy of Rome Diocese (February 22, 2007)

223. Looking

Looking at Christ, we feel at the same time looked at by him.

Angelus (February 25, 2007)

March 2007

224. Angels

These angels can fly because they are not regulated by the gravity of the earth's material things but by the gravity of the Risen One's love; and that we would be able to fly if we were to step outside material gravity and enter the new gravity of the love of the Risen One.

Address, Lenten retreat for Roman Curia (March 3, 2007)

225. Answer

Behind so many phenomena of our time that appear to be very far from religion and from Christ, there is a question, an expectation, a desire; and that the one true response to this ever-present desire precisely in our time is Christ.

Address, Lenten retreat for Roman Curia (March 3, 2007)

226. True prayer

True prayer consists precisely in uniting our will with that of God.

Angelus (March 4, 2007)

227. God and Caesar

Caesar is not everything. Another sovereignty emerges whose origins and essence are not of this world but of "the heavens above": it is that of Truth, which also claims a right to be heard by the State.

General audience (March 7, 2007)

228. The shadows of communication

Much of what is transmitted [by mass media] in various forms to the homes of millions of families around the world is destructive. By directing the light of Christ's truth upon such shadows the Church engenders hope.

Address to Pontifical Council for Social Communications
(March 9, 2007)

229. Scientia Crucis

Christian wisdom is the wisdom of the Cross.

Greeting at the Rosary with university students
(March 10, 2007)

230. Conversion

Conversion overcomes the root of evil, which is sin, even if it cannot always avoid its consequences.

Angelus (March 11, 2007)

231. Like Mary

Mary of Nazareth, icon of the nascent Church, is the model for each of us, called to receive the gift that Jesus makes of himself in the Eucharist.

Apostolic Exhortation Sacramentum Caritatis
(published March 13, 2007; n. 33)

232. *Iuxta dominicam vivere*

"Living in accordance with the Lord's Day" (Saint Ignatius of Antioch) means living in the awareness of the liberation brought by Christ and making our lives a constant self-offering to God, so that his victory may be fully revealed to all humanity through a profoundly renewed existence.

Apostolic Exhortation Sacramentum Caritatis (n. 72)

233. Priestly spirituality

The priest should make his spiritual life his highest priority. He is called to seek God tirelessly, while remaining attuned to the concerns of his brothers and sisters.

Apostolic Exhortation Sacramentum Caritatis (n. 80)

234. Moral transformation

The moral urgency born of welcoming Jesus into our lives is the fruit of gratitude for having experienced the Lord's unmerited closeness.

Apostolic Exhortation Sacramentum Caritatis (n. 82)

235. The witness

We become witnesses when, through our actions, words and way of being, Another makes himself present.

Apostolic Exhortation Sacramentum Caritatis (n. 85)

236. Bearing Christ

[The task of the mission of the Christian people is to bring Christ.] Not just a theory or a way of life inspired by Christ, but the gift of his very person.

Apostolic Exhortation Sacramentum Caritatis (n. 87)

237. The social role of the Church

It is not the proper task of the Church to engage in the political work of bringing about the most just society possible; nonetheless she cannot and must not remain on the sidelines in the struggle for justice.
Apostolic Exhortation Sacramentum Caritatis (n. 89)

238. The works of God

God likes to carry out his works using poor means. He therefore asks you to make a generous faith available to him!
Address to pilgrims (March 17, 2007)

239. The sense of humanity

Life without God does not work; it lacks the essential, it lacks light, it lacks reason, it lacks the great sense of being human.
Homily, Rome's Prison for Minors (March 18, 2007)

240. With others

The human being is not a "monad", an isolated being who lives only for himself and must have life for himself alone. On the contrary, we live with others, we were created together with others and only in being with others, in giving ourselves to others, do we find life.
Homily, Rome's Prison for Minors (March 18, 2007)

241. The questions of a theologian

First of all, we have to ask questions. Those who do not ask do not get a reply. But I would add that

84

for theology, in addition to the courage to ask, we also need the humility to listen to the answers that the Christian faith gives us.
Meeting, Faculty of Theology, Tubingen (March 21, 2007)

242. The apostasy of Europe

Is it not surprising that today's Europe, while aspiring to be regarded as a community of values, seems ever more often to deny the very existence of universal and absolute values? Does not this unique form of "apostasy" from itself, even more than its apostasy from God, lead Europe to doubt its own identity?
Address to the Congress 'Values and Perspectives for Tomorrow's Europe - 50 years of the Treaty of Rome'
(March 24, 2007)

243. Thirst

In the heart of every man, begging for love, there is a thirst for love.
Homily, Penitential Celebration with the Youth of the Diocese of Rome (March 29, 2007)

244. Witnesses of charity

It is not simply a question of becoming more "competitive" and "productive", but it is necessary to be "witnesses of charity".
Message 9th International Youth Forum
(March 30, 2007)

Index